rourkeeducationalmedia.com

Rourke
Educational Media

Kay Robertson

Calculating Time

www.rourkeeducationalmedia.com

PHOTO CREDITS:Cover; ©; XXX, 1; © CaraMaria, 4; © Vasilius, STILLFX, 5; © Oguzaral, © Tarajane, 6; © Jeff Gynane, 7; © mbbirdy, 8; © Muhla1, miklavv, 9; © anaken2012, 10; © aceshot, 11; © Andrew_Howe, tykhyi, 12; © Yagello Oleksandra, 13; © Pedro Monteiro, 14; © xxx, Jim David, 15; © ziggymaj, 16; © FrankRamspott, 17; © Eitak, chris_lemmens, 18; © Eitak, Creative Commons, 19; © dell640, 20; © ISerg, 21; © Claudio Divizia, 22; © Lightspring, 23; © Alexander Levin , 24; © alan64, 25; © chrysh, Hunor Focze, 26; © filo, 27; © xxx, Igor Leshchinski, 28; © Igor Leshchinski , 29; © Orientaly, 30; © Zurijeta, 32; © Pressmaster, 34; © _human, 35; © sculpies, 36; © Creative Commons, 37; © jessicaphoto, 38; © antoninaart, 39; © sneska, 40; © Anastasios71, 41; © Vjom, 42; © GlobalStock, 44; © Nmint

Edited by: Jill Sherman

Cover by: Renee Brady
Interior design by: Cory Davis

Library of Congress PCN Data

STEM Guides to Calculating Time / Kay Robertson.
    p. cm. -- (STEM Everyday)
Includes index.
ISBN 978-1-62169-850-0 (hardcover)
ISBN 978-1-62169-745-9 (softcover)
ISBN 978-1-62169-953-8 (e-Book)
Library of Congress Control Number: 2013936456

Also Available as:

Rourke Educational Media
Printed in the United States of America,
North Mankato, Minnesota

Rourke
Educational Media

rourkeeducationalmedia.com

customerservice@rourkeeducationalmedia.com • PO Box 643328 Vero Beach, Florida 32964

Table of Contents

Introduction

Time is difficult to define, but it happens all day, every day. By keeping track of time we know when to get up in the morning, when summer vacation starts, and when to buy presents for an upcoming holiday.

Time is so vast that in order to deal with it, human beings have to divide it up into small portions: years, weeks, months, hours, minutes, seconds.

Time is happening all the time!

In this book we will look at all of those time **segments.** You will also learn how much math can be done with time.

STEM in Action

Have you ever made a family timeline? It can be a fun project to work on with your parents and siblings. A family timeline shows when each person in the family was born. Depending on how far back you want to go, you can even show grandparents and great-grandparents.

Let's imagine some dates. For instance, say you were born in 2001. Picture your family timeline. If you had a relative who died in 1965, how many years passed between that person's death and your birth?

You can find out by subtracting the smaller number from the larger number:

2001 − 1965 = 36

There were 36 years between your relative's death and your birth!

Child
Birth – 2001

Parent
Birth – 1967

Grandparent
Birth – 1947

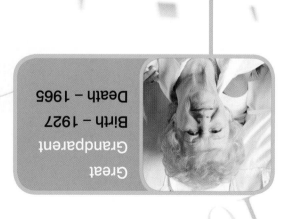

Great
Grandparent
Birth – 1927
Death – 1965

Using Clocks

Clocks are all around us. Some clocks are part of something else, like the clock in an automatic coffee maker. Some clocks are so big that they become symbols of an entire country, like Big Ben in London, England. You may even be wearing a clock on one of your wrists in the form of a watch.

One of the most famous analog clocks in the world is Big Ben. At what time was this picture of Big Ben taken?

Clocks are also a good example of how people use math every single day.

Most of the clocks that people see and use today are **digital**. All this means is that digital clocks display only the digits needed to express the correct time. Not long ago, though, another kind of clock was popular. It was the **analog** clock.

STEM in Action ?

Let's say that you have an appointment with the dentist at 4:30 p.m. Now, imagine that the current time is 1:00 p.m.

How much time do you have until your appointment with the dentist?

4:30 – 1:00 = 3:30

You have 3 hours and 30 minutes until your dentist appointment!

Digital clocks like this one display the numbers of the time individually.

STEM in Action ?

You may be wondering why an analog clock only includes the numbers 1 through 12. This is because the hour hand on the clock goes through two full rotations each day:

$$12 + 12 = 24$$

If there are 24 hours in a day, how many minutes are there in a day?

First, you need to know that every hour is divided into 60 minutes. Now it's just a matter of using multiplication:

$$24 \times 60 = 1,440$$

Now how about seconds?

Again, every minute is divided into 60 seconds. There are actually two ways to solve this problem. You could multiply the number of minutes in a day by the number of seconds per minute:

$$1,440 \times 60 = 86,400$$

There are 1,440 minutes in a day!

Or, you could multiply the number of seconds in an hour by the number of hours in a day.

$$60 \times 60 = 3,600$$

There are 3,600 seconds in an hour.

$$3,600 \times 24 = 86,400$$

Either way, the result is the same. There are 86,400 seconds in a day.

Analog clocks take a little more time to read than digital clocks, but they aren't really so complicated. A day is divided into hours, minutes, and seconds.

A day is the amount of time that the Earth takes to experience one rotation on its **axis**. This is done in a period of 24 hours.

An analog clock has three hands. Each of the three hands points to a specific thing. Now that you've learned how to calculate the number of minutes and number of seconds in a period of time, you can see why we don't speak about time like this. It takes too long to figure out, and the numbers are too big. But they are useful examples of understanding how we divide a day.

STEM Fast Fact !

Subdivisions

Believe it or not, a second is not the smallest portion of time that exists.

There are even smaller units of time such as:

1 centisecond = 1 hundredth of a second = 0.01

1 millisecond = 1 thousandth of a second = 0.001

1 microsecond = 1 millionth of a second = 0.000001

1 nanosecond = 1 billionth of a second = 0.000000001

In everyday life these units aren't really needed. They are often used by scientists for studying things like chemical reactions or the speed of light.

Precise clocks like this stopwatch measure smaller increments of time, such as divisions of a second.

Using Military Time

Ordinary citizens think of time differently than people in the military. This is because members of the military use military time.

From flight maneuvers to training exercises, everything the military does depends on precision.

You may already be familiar with military time from movies, television, or the news. Maybe you've heard a soldier or general refer to *oh-eight hundred hours* or *sixteen hundred hours*. What do those terms mean?

In order to understand military time, you first need to take a step backward. Remember that standard clocks include only the numbers 1 through 12. They make up for it by going through two rotations. Depending on what time of day it is, it is usually simple to figure out whether the clock is referring to a.m. (morning) or p.m. (evening).

A 24-hour clock really isn't that different from a standard clock. If they are set properly, both clocks will tell the correct time of day, just in different ways. In standard time, 9 o'clock in the morning is expressed as *oh-nine hundred hours* in military time. Military time only starts to become different from regular time after noon.

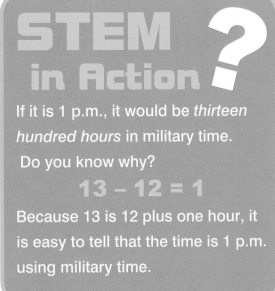

STEM in Action?

If it is 1 p.m., it would be *thirteen hundred hours* in military time. Do you know why?

$$13 - 12 = 1$$

Because 13 is 12 plus one hour, it is easy to tell that the time is 1 p.m. using military time.

For periods after noon, translating military time to civilian time is easy. All you have to do is subtract 12 from the military time. More precisely, you'll want to subtract 1200 hours from the military time in order to figure out how many hours after noon the military time is referring to.

STEM ? in Action

Since the military clock goes through a 24-hour cycle, time is expressed using the number of hours that have passed since midnight. Military time also uses 4 digits to express any time.

0100 = Oh-one hundred hours = 1 a.m

But can you convert these times to military time?

1700 = 17 hundred hours
2100 = 21 hundred hours

Can you convert those military times to civilian time? Start with the first one:

1700 – 1200 = 500

Seventeen hundred hours is just another way of saying 5 p.m.!

Try the next one:

2100 – 1200 = 900

Twenty-one hundred hours is 9 p.m.!

Finally, what is *twenty-four hundred hours*?

2400 – 1200 = 1,200

Twenty-four hundred hours is 12 midnight!

STEM
Fast Fact

Sundials

Sundials, or shadow clocks, are one of the first timepieces. The gnomon is the pointer on a sundial that casts the shadow. It is a word that comes from ancient Greek and means "indicator." Sundials work by the sun casting a shadow on the sundial's gnomon. When the Sun is at it highest point of the day, or midday, the shadow is the shortest. When the Sun is lower, in the afternoon, the shadow is the longest.

It is important to keep in mind that the Sun's height is also affected by the seasons. Sundials are usually well marked with daylight hours, and there are some that have all 24 hours marked on them.

The Leaning Tower of Pisa, in Italy. If it was 2 p.m. standard time when this picture was taken, what was it in military time?

All About Time Zones

Do you have cousins who live in another part of the United States? Or maybe you have friends who live overseas in another country. If so, then you probably already have some knowledge of time zones.

Different parts of the world experience different times. In the same way that a day is divided into 24 hours, the Earth is divided into 24 different time zones. Part of the reason for time zones has to do with the position of the Sun in relation to Earth. For each time zone, the Sun will be at its highest point in the sky at precisely 12 noon.

Can You Find Your Time Zone?

The Greenwich Meridian separates east from west in the same way that the Equator separates north from south.

The starting point for these zones is in Greenwich, England. Depending on whether or not a location is east or west of an imaginary line, called the Greenwich Meridian, determines if a time zone is plus or minus a set number of hours.

Although it sounds complicated, the main thing to understand is that each time zone is different from the next by exactly one hour. In the continental United States alone there are four time zones. From east to west they are Eastern, Central, Mountain, and Pacific. If you are going from east to west, each of these time zones is less one hour.

STEM in Action ?

If it is noon in the Eastern time zone, what time is it in the Central time zone?

$$12 - 1 = 11$$

It is 11 a.m. in the Central zone. And what about in the Mountain and Pacific regions?

Mountain: $11 - 1 = 10$ a.m.

Pacific: $10 - 1 = 9$ a.m.

STEM in Action ?

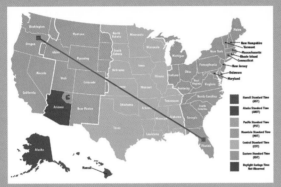

Calling Oregon to Florida

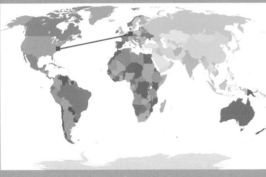

North Carolina to Germany

How about this? Imagine that you live somewhere in the state of Oregon (Pacific zone). It is 5 p.m. Let's say you want to call a friend who lives in Florida (Eastern zone). What time will it be in Florida?

It's easy to figure out. Just remember that the Eastern zone would be three hours *ahead* of the Pacific zone:

$$5 + 3 = 8$$

So if it's 5 p.m. in Oregon, it's 8 p.m. in Florida!

Let's try another problem using a different country. To solve this problem you need to use a little military time.

Germany is 6 hours ahead of states in the Eastern time zone.

If you are in North Carolina and it is 7:30 a.m., what time is it in Germany?

$$7:30 + 6 = 13:30$$

And to convert that to standard time, just subtract 1200 hours:

$$1330 - 1200 = 130$$

When it is 7:30 a.m. in North Carolina, it is 1:30 p.m. in Germany!

Alaska

California

Because it is so far west, Alaska is in the Alaska time zone, which is one hour earlier than the Pacific zone. If it is 5 p.m. in California, what time is it in Alaska?

Depending on the locations you're dealing with, time zones can become rather confusing. For one thing, there is another imaginary line like the Greenwich Meridian on the opposite side of the Earth. This line is situated roughly over the middle of the Pacific Ocean. It is called the International Date Line, and where you are in relation to it determines what day it is. If you travel eastward over the line, you lose one day. Traveling westward over the International Date Line adds a day.

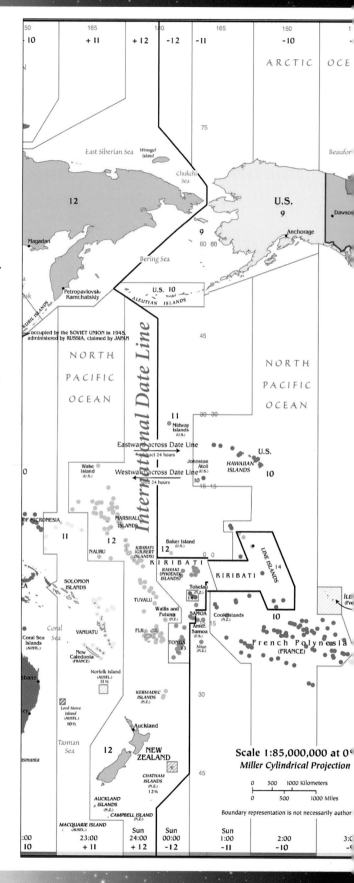

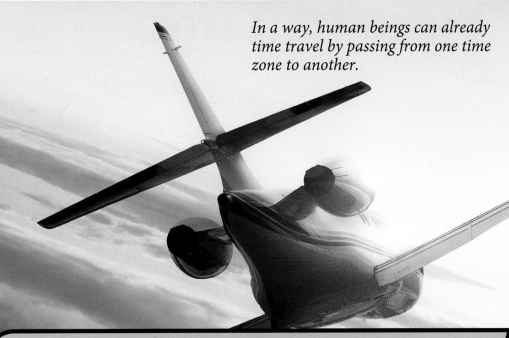

In a way, human beings can already time travel by passing from one time zone to another.

STEM Fast Fact !

Daylight Savings Time

Like time zones, another quirk of time we deal with in the modern world is Daylight Savings Time.

Daylight Savings Time has been with us since World War I. Daylight Savings Time is only an adjustment of one hour. It takes advantage of the extra sunlight that we have in the summer. Daylight Savings Time takes place every year between the first Sunday in April until the last Sunday in October.

Not everyone in the United States uses Daylight Savings Time. People in Arizona do not reset their clocks, and in some states, some places use Daylight Savings Time and some don't.

So imagine it is a summer day in Massachusetts, exactly 2 p.m. What time will it be in Arizona? Don't forget to adjust for time zones!

A Year in Time

Just as a single day can be divided into different segments, so can a year.

You don't often hear people talking about the number of hours in a year. More commonly, people divide a year into segments like months, weeks, and days.

Whether it is a leap year or not, February is always the shortest month.

February 2014

SUN	MON	TUE	WED	THU	FRI	SAT
26	27	28	29	30	31	1
2	3	4	5	6	7	8
9	10	11	12	13	14	15
16	17	18	19	20	21	22
23	24	25	26	27	28	1

January 2014

Months are a collection of between 28 to 31 days. Using those figures, you can calculate the **average** length of a month.

STEM in Action ?

Now do the same thing for the number of days in a month:

$$28 + 31 = 59$$
$$59 \div 2 = 29.5$$

And just to make things easier, round the result up to 30. The average length of a month is about 30 days!

Knowing that, can you find out how many months there are in a year? You can find out by dividing the number of days in a year by the average length of a month:

$$365 \div 30 = 12.16$$

Just to keep things neat, you can drop the digits to the right of the decimal point. Now you can say that there are 12 months in a year!

Remember that averages are not **absolute**. Just because the average length of a month is 30 days does not mean that every month lasts thirty days. Some months are shorter than 30 days. Some are longer. Rather, the average here is a way of saying that each month in a year lasts around 30 days.

Monday

1

Tuesday

2

Wednesday

3

Thursday

4

Friday

5

Saturday

6

Sunday

7

STEM ? in Action

Let's try something else. Do you know how many days there are in a week? You can figure it out just by reciting them and giving each one a number:

Monday – 1
Tuesday – 2
Wednesday – 3
Thursday – 4
Friday – 5
Saturday – 6
Sunday – 7

There are 7 days in a week!

STEM
in Action ?

Now the question is, how many weeks are there in a year?

You can find out by using division:

$$365 ÷ 7 = 52.2$$

Once again, you can drop the numbers to the right of the decimal point. You now know that there are 52 weeks in a year.

The number of days in a month or year can change, but the number of days in a week is always the same!

STEM Fast Fact !

Leap Years

Actually, a year is slightly more than 365 days. In fact, one year is precisely equal to 365 days, 5 hours, 48 minutes, and 46 seconds. That is the exact length of a solar year, or the period of time it takes the Earth to revolve around the Sun.

What happens to all that extra time?

To compensate for those missing hours, the concept of the leap year was developed. Every fourth year is a leap year with a full extra day that takes place on February 29. If you didn't already know, 2012 was a leap year!

After 2012, what are the next three leaps year be?

$$2012 + 4 = 2016$$
$$2016 + 4 = 2020$$
$$2020 + 4 = 2024$$

2016, 2020, and 2024 are leap years.

Working with Calendars

Dividing the year into months, weeks, and days is part of making a **calendar**. A calendar is very much like a watch in that it is a tool people use to keep track of time. Calendars differ from watches in that they measure much longer periods of time.

The type of calendar you are probably familiar with is the Gregorian calendar. The Gregorian calendar has been in use for hundreds of years. Its periods are based on the movements of the Earth around the Sun. Remember that there are 365 days in a year. It takes the Earth 365 days to revolve once around the Sun!

You might be surprised to know that many people use more than one calendar. Chinese people use a calendar that also lasts 365 days, but on the Chinese calendar, the year 2013 is actually 4710!

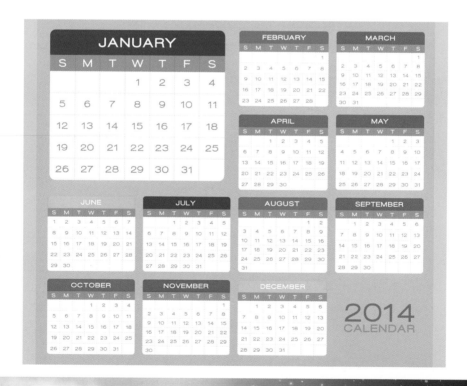

二月

蛇 SNAKE

贰零 壹叁 **2013**

FEBRUARY

日 SUN	一 MON	二 TUE	三 WED	四 THU	五 FRI	六 SAT
					01	02
03	04	05	06	07	08	09
10	11	12	13	14	15	16
17	18	19	20	21	22	23
24	25	26	27	28		

Because the Chinese calendar is based on the moon rather than the Sun, New Year's Day always falls on a different date.

YEAR:	2013	2014	2015	2016	2107
Gregorian Calendar New Year	January 1	January 1	January 1	January 1	January 1
Chinese Calendar New Year	March 2	January 31	February 19	February 8	January 28

2012

אפריל	מרץ	פברואר	ינואר
אוגוסט	יולי	יוני	מאי
דצמבר	נובמבר	אוקטובר	ספטמבר

Jewish people use a calendar that is based on the moon rather than the Sun. The Jewish calendar is divided into 12 months just like the Gregorian calendar. However, the months of the Jewish calendar have different names and an extra month is included every 19 years.

Sound confusing? It really isn't. In fact, you probably use different calendars all the time. You might think of January 1 as the first day of a new year, but the first day of a new school year could be sometime in late August.

In the business world, most companies have a fiscal year that might begin at any time on a standard calendar. The end of a fiscal year is when the company does its accounting. Business people also often divide a standard year into quarters. The word quarter is an expression of the fraction 1/4.

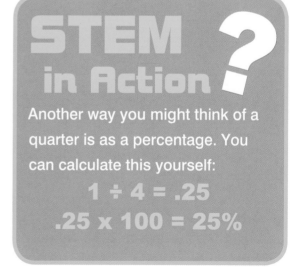

STEM in Action?

Another way you might think of a quarter is as a percentage. You can calculate this yourself:

$$1 \div 4 = .25$$
$$.25 \times 100 = 25\%$$

Businesses like farming and agriculture are extremely dependent on the calendar because some crops only grow at certain times of the year.

STEM in Action ?

If there are 12 months in a year, what would a quarter of a year be?

$$12 \div 4 = 3$$

A quarter of a year is equal to three months!

What about weeks? How many weeks are there in a quarter of a year?

$$52 \div 4 = 13$$

There are 13 weeks in a quarter year!

And finally, how many days are there in a quarter of a year?

$$365 \div 4 = 91.3$$

There are about 91 days in a quarter of a year!

Dividing the year into quarters makes it easier for businesses to keep track of earnings.

The division of a year into quarters is mainly for the convenience of dealing with smaller chunks of time. It is also useful for making **predictions** about the future.

STEM in Action ?

Since we know that a quarter of a year is divided into chunks of three months, let's divide a calendar into quarters:

Quarter 1:	Quarter 2:	Quarter 3:	Quarter 4:
January	April	July	October
February	May	August	November
March	June	September	December

Now imagine that you are working for a company. In the first quarter of the year, your company earned $2,500. In the second quarter of the year, your company earned $3,250. In the third quarter, the company earned $4,100.

Using those figures, can you determine the average company earnings per quarter?

$$2,500 + 3,250 + 4,100 = 9,850$$
$$9,850 \div 3 = 3,283$$

The average company earnings for a quarter are about $3,283!
Meanwhile, you may have noticed that for each quarter, the amount of money the company earned went up slightly:

Quarter 1	Quarter 2	Quarter 3
$2,500	$3,250	$4,100

This is where you can make a prediction. Since each quarter the company earned a little more, it is reasonable to think that in the fourth quarter, the company earnings will be more than the third quarter total of $4,100.

Now you know why business people find a year divided into quarters useful.

STEM Fast Fact!

Days of the Month

Every month has about 29 or 30 days. But what is the exact number of days in each month?

Here's a simple rhyme you can use to remember:

"Thirty days has September
April, June, and November;
All the rest have thirty-one.
Except February alone,
And that has twenty-eight days clear
And twenty-nine in each leap year."

Knowing that, can you say how many more days there are in November compared to February? What about compared to February in a leap year?

September 2014

S	M	T	W	T	F	S
	1	2	3	4	5	6
7	8	9	10	11	12	13
14	15	16	17	18	19	20
21	22	23	24	25	26	27
28	29	30				

April 2014

S	M	T	W	T	F	S
		1	2	3	4	5
6	7	8	9	10	11	12
13	14	15	16	17	18	19
20	21	22	23	24	25	26
27	28	29	30			

June 2014

S	M	T	W	T	F	S
1	2	3	4	5	6	7
8	9	10	11	12	13	14
15	16	17	18	19	20	21
22	23	24	25	26	27	28
29	30					

February 2014

S	M	T	W	T	F	S
						1
2	3	4	5	6	7	8
9	10	11	12	13	14	15
16	17	18	19	20	21	22
23	24	25	26	27	28	

November 2014

S	M	T	W	T	F	S
						1
2	3	4	5	6	7	8
9	10	11	12	13	14	15
16	17	18	19	20	21	22
23	24	25	26	27	28	29
30						

What's the Difference?

This book you are reading was published in the year 2014. But to be precise, it was published in the year AD 2014. The AD is an abbreviation of the phrase Anno Domini. Anno Domini is Latin for "in the year of the Lord."

The Great Sphinx, in Egypt. This civilization existed before the year 1.

The factors that made the Gregorian calendar what it is today include a mix of the scientific and the religious. Scientifically, the calendar is based on the revolutions of the Earth around both the Sun and its own axis. Religion, on the other hand, is why we are actually in a year called Anno Domini.

There is no zero year in the Gregorian calendar. Instead, the year 1 is said to be the year of Christ's birth. Anytime after that is Anno Domini. Meanwhile, anytime before year 1 is dated B.C.E. BC is an abbreviation for "Before Christ." B.C.E. means "Before the Common Era." It is used by non-Christians or those not wishing to refer to religious events.

What happened before the year 1? Dinosaurs roamed the Earth and were eventually wiped out by some form of catastrophe. Ancient peoples built monuments like Stonehenge in England. One of the world's first great civilizations developed in Egypt.

STEM in Action?

Finding out how much time has passed in terms of Anno Domini years is simple.

For instance, World War II ended in 1945. How many years passed between the end of World War II and when you were born?
Let's say you were born in 1996:

$$1996 - 1945 = 51$$

51 years passed between the end of World War II and your birth.
Do you know the solution to this problem?

$$-23 + -7 = ?$$

But how do we deal with dates B.C.E.? What if you were interested in figuring out how many years it has been since Alexander the Great became king of Macedonia in 336 B.C.E.?

Before you solve that problem, let's talk a bit about **negative** numbers.

Telling time is one of the oldest human inventions. Humankind's efforts to tell time have helped drive the evolution of our technology and science throughout history.

When you add two negative numbers together, the result is negative as well.

Working with B.C.E. time is a bit like working with negative numbers. Instead of subtracting years from the current date, you're going to add them.

STEM in Action ?

In order to solve this problem, you need to understand that all numbers, positive or negative, have an absolute value. To find out the absolute value of a number, just remove the sign. So, the absolute value of -23 is 23. Likewise, the absolute value of -7 is 7.

$$23 + 7 = 30$$

So, if Alexander the Great became king of Macedonia in 336 B.C.E. and the current year is 2014, how many years are between those two dates?

$$336 + 2014 = 2,350$$

It has been 2,350 years since Alexander the Great became king of Macedonia!

Try This

The Chinese philosopher Lao-tse was born in the year 604 BC. We can also say that he was born in 604 B.C.E.

How many years passed between Lao-tse's birth and yours? Now, see how many years passed between the following famous inventors birthdays and yours.

Eli Whitney 1765

Alexander Graham Bell 1847

Do you know what these famous people in history invented?

You can trace the development of technologies, from the first phones invented in the 1870s to the cell phone you keep in your pocket, developed in 1989.

Conclusion

What time is it right now? What time was it when you started reading this book? Can you figure out how long it took you to read this book?

At some point in your life it may occur to you that you'd like to stop time or maybe even reverse it. Maybe you'll have a big school project due and not enough time to prepare. Maybe you'll go on a family vacation and have so much fun that you'll wish you could live it all again.

Time is always passing, so make each day count!

Time keeps on going. The only direction time knows is forward. With a little math you can learn to use it to your advantage. Just remember, time is all about the past, present, and the future.

What are you planning to do with your time?

Glossary

absolute (AB-suh-loot): the pure value of a number, regardless of whether it is positive or negative

addends (AD-ends): the numbers added together in an addition problem

analog (AN-uh-lawg): data in a continuous wave

average (AV-ur-ij): a number used to represent a group of numbers

axis (AK-sis): a straight line through the center of a round body; the point around which the Earth spins

calendar (KAL-uhn-dur): a device or system used for measuring a year of time

digital (DIJ-i-tuhl): data broken down into small portions

negative (NEG-uh-tiv): with a value less than zero

predictions (pri-DIKT-shuhns): imagining a likely outcome

segments (SEG-muhntz): small parts of something bigger

Index

Time Zone Map

"When it's 8:00 a.m. in Greenwich, it's ..."

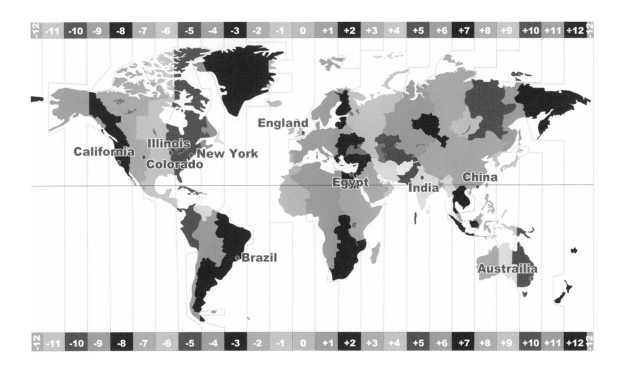

10:00 a.m. in Cairo, Egypt

9:00 a.m. in London, England

5:00 a.m. in Rio de Janiero, Brazil

4:00 a.m. in New York City, NY

3:00 a.m. in Chicago, Illinois

2:00 a.m. in Denver, Colorado

1:00 a.m. in Los Angeles, California

6:00 p.m. in Sydney, Australia

1:30 p.m. in New Delhi, India

4:00 p.m. in Hong Kong, China

Websites to Visit

classroom.jc-schools.net/basic/math-time.html

kidsblogs.nationalgeographic.com/2009/10/27/what-is-daylight-
savings-time-anyway

www.spacearchive.info/military.htm

Show What You Know

1. How often do leap years happen?

2. Which type of calendar do we use in the United States?

3. If you live in Ohio and traveled to California, how many time
zones would you cross?

4. Why is military time different?

5. Calculate how many years older your teacher is compared to you.